Table of Contents

1. A Very Special Lady
2. Remember Me
3. Talk Is Cheap
4. Nothing Compare To You
5. Cindy's Pain
6. In A Better Place
7. Believe
8. Choose Life
9. My Boys
10. Thank You
11. Before You Cheat
12. Farewell
13. My Mistake
14. Two-Face
15. Still Choosing Life
16. Thank God For Small Treasures
17. Your Man
18. Leave It To Fate
19. K.T.F For Life
20. If I'd Told Her No
21. This World Would Be
22. Mountain..Get out of my Way
23. Can You Feel The Love?
24. Do Not Weep For Me
25. Tougher Than Nails
26. The Dilemma
27. Don't Say Good-Bye
28. Just A Thought Away

29. *A Dream Come True*
30. *The Grey Soldiers*
31. *Home For Christmas*
32. *Flaws and All*
33. *In The Hood*
34. *The True O.G.*
35. *The Seduction*
36. *Another Try*
37. *What Goes Around*
38. *They Grow Fast*
39. *Forever and a Day*
40. *Remember The Time*
41. *On My Mama*
42. *Second To None*
43. *Tribute To Mom*

This book is dedicated to my fiancée DeLinda, for believing in me. My kids Chase, Vincent, Hunter, and Ariel for being such inspirations to me. My School Teachers from School 52, Southport Middle, South Wayne Jr. High, and Ben Davis High School for their input and teachings. For my Mother Glenda, for giving me this passion for writing. And to my family and friends for being there for me. Thank you all.

A Very Special Lady

Every time I think of this lady
Who is always on my mind
The one to spend my time, with
a very special lady

This lady I know who is sweet and nice
She's is truly pure sugar and spice
Her hair is long, body slender
Skin is soft, and lips ever so tender

This lady is always on my mind
I only wish that she was mine
Like a lovely red rose, coming up on
spring day
I've never seen true beauty, until I saw
her that first day

Remember Me

Months have gone by since I've seen your face

Not being able to leave this wired fence place

And I know you may be busy, with six kids by your side

Making all those lunches, and finding keys they hide

But before you go insane from kids yelling and things

Please take time to sit for a moment and remember me

The very first kiss I gave you underneath the stars

The long hour trips we took, in each other's cars

The time we spent cuddling, while watching the big screen T.V

Or massaging you with lotion, from your head down to your feet

I know I cannot be there to put your mind at ease

So take this time to smile a while and remember me

Being locked up in this facility causes my heart to hurt

Cause I think about my new son, that will soon be blessing this earth

And you having to deliver without me at your side

Breaks me down even more, to where I could easily die

And although the pain will be unbearable when the doctor says "On three"

When you push say a prayer, and remember me

Doing time in this prison is hard enough without my girl at my side

Or not being able to kiss my kids, when they go to bed at night

At times like these I turn to God, to help me through the day

So late at night I bow my head, and this is what I say

"There are millions of people with millions of problems, and they all come to you on praying knees

But if you have time in your busy schedule, oh Lord, I ask of you to remember me."

Talk Is Cheap....When It Comes To Love

Love comes in many ways to people in this world
Love is shown by all genders adults, boys, and girls
Love comes in many colors white, black, or blue
It doesn't matter what color you are, as long as your love is true
So don't let others tell you wrong, use your heart as a guide
You can't choose love from the color of skin, it comes from the feeling inside
They say beauty is in the eye of the beholder, and love is always blind
And if your love is truly pure, it will last a long, long time
So don't let others steer you wrong, whenever your paths come to meet
Just tell them the truth, when it comes to love talk..... Is cheap

Nothing Compares To You

I've heard a dolphins cry for help, and seen a babies eyes weep

I've seen an eagle flying high over mountain tops, whose sides run down so deep

I've seen the sun rise high over the horizon, and settle down in the west

But of all the wonderful things I've seen, sweetheart you're still the best

The sky is cute I must admit, and the sea is pretty too.

And I've never seen in a rose or flower, a lovelier shade of blue

There are many more things in this world I know, that are blessed with beauty to

But they could never in a million years, be able to compare to you.

Cindy's Pain

A tragic loss, so I am called

Is what they say, down in the halls

A car door slammed, and my father came in

He just lost his job, and had been drinking gin

He yells out my name, I do not come

For the many times it has happened, this may be the one

He stumbles up the stairs, and slams open my door

I lay quietly in fear and horror, keeping still on the bedroom floor

He lifts up my bed, and grab me by the hair

And said when he calls my name, I better be right there

He beats me and hits me, it does not ease

"Oh God I beg you, stop the pain... Please!!"

There was a sudden silence, I do not know why

But a strange glowing figure, came in front of my eyes

My name is Cindy, I was only three
When my father came home and murdered me

In A Better Place

I watched this young boy, lying peacefully, in a coffin he died from illnesses at birth

And as I sat and listen to the services, I thought about what he'll miss here on earth

Like the smell of spring on a clear sunny day (Just over-look the factory pollution that goes rolling by)

Or school kids playing on a see-saw at recess (although these days they play with guns and knives)

Going walking in a park or downtown (look out for the robbers and rapist at night)

Or even just sitting on the porch reading a good book (Be sure to duck when the gangs start to shoot and fight)

As I walk to the coffin to pay my last respects, I noticed he had left us with a smile

He must be playing catch with the angels right now, and walking on the fluffy white clouds

As I walked away I can't help but recall, all the crime I see everywhere

And I realized just then why the boy was smiling, he's is in a far better place with the man upstairs

Believe

A young boy asked his mother one day, as she started to clean

"How do you know that God is real, if he cannot be seen?"

So the mother sat the little boy down, next to her on her bed

She thought real hard about how to answer, and this is what she said

"The wind that blows on your face, or the love you feel for me

Cannot be held in the palm of your hand, nor with eyes can you see

Sometimes you just know that things are real, no matter what people say

That's the way god is, you feel him in your heart, each and every day"

The curious boy looked at his mom and said "Do you believe in God too?"

She said "Yes" With a smile, and pointed at him "Because he brought me you"

Choose Life

Hear ye, hear ye…. And hear ye, well

For I have something to say, that I must tell

This is to all the boys and girls, ladies and gents, and to those who are husbands and wives

The subject is Abortion; the reason is simple everyone has a right to life

To live a long life that's full of love, is all any human-being ever wants

Maybe to go shopping with their mom at the mall, or in the forest with dad on a hunt

The intimate times that you spend with your lover, or even when conception occurs

Can all be described as a moment of "love", which sums up the baby in a word

A child does not ask to be brought into this world, nor does he ask to leave

But when life is forming inside your body, God would want it to continue, guaranteed

Life is precious to everything: to the plants, the animals, and little kids too.

And if any doubt still remains in your mind about choosing life, just remember that your mom did…. With you

My Boys

My kids were at the park one day, playing with a couple of boys
And one kid with a green action figure stood up with his toy
He said "The Hulk is the strongest man there is" and my son Chase then stood to say
"He may be strong but my dad's stronger on any given day
He can run faster than The Flash can, and beat super-man one-on-one
Why he can lift an elephant with one hand, and those things must weigh a ton
Yeah I know you think I'm crazy, and that I've gone plum mad
But the Incredible hulk may be strong, but not as strong as my dad

Well another kid stood and did a backwards flip
"Can your dad do that?" he said

This time Vincent stood proudly yelling, "That was pretty cool, but not as cool as my dad

He can skydive from an Air-o- plane, and swim in the biggest lakes

And you should have seen him boy back when he had that 20 feet snake

Now you can say what you want, say I'm crazy and even call me mad

But you may be cool with that little flip, but not as cool as my dad"

As a father I've made my share of mistakes, while taking care of the kids, you see

But in their eyes I can do no wrong, because they have that much love for me

Oh sure you're probably saying every son and daughter, is a parent's bundle of joy

And that may be true, your kids are good, but not as great as my boys

Thank You

The glare in your eyes, when you look at me

The touch of your hands, upon my cheek

The tender kiss of your lips, meeting mines

And the love that is made, when our bodies intertwine

All of these things are bonuses, to what I truly adore

Which is the little things you do, that makes me love you more

Like calling to say I love you, just minutes after I leave the house

And even though you hate the color, you'll wear my favorite blouse

When I was sick you took care of me, and never once complained

And set out an umbrella by the door, when it was going to rain

So far all the things you may have given up, or had to sacrifice

Just know that I love you, and I thank you dearly for being in my life

Before You Cheat

To all the men who has a woman, and another or a wife

Take heed and listen to what I say because it may just save your life

A man and his girl was out on a date at a local pizza place

While his girlfriend was back at home cleaning up his place

She found a note dated yesterday, and a pair of women's underwear

Neither of which belong to her and the rage was too much to bare

The young man came home from his so called late work, and as he opened the door

He noticed all his clothes ripped to pieces, scattered on the floor

His 52' inch T.V was smashed to bits, his couch was torn to shreds

And what could only be described as formaldehyde covered his entire bed

He was shocked and hurt and fell to the floor, then grab his heart in pain

And as he walked back to his front door he notices the letter with his name

"You've lost your most prize possessions your furniture and T.V

I left you your girlfriend's letter and underwear, on the table you will see

I redecorated your house just like you asked, I hope you like what you see

Maybe next time you will think twice before cheating on me"

Men hell has no fury like a woman scorned, and it is doubled when she has proof

And if she catches you in one too many lies her rage will hit the roof

So weigh the price of what you will lose, if you got with the girl down the street

It could cost you your house or maybe your life, so think before you cheat

Farewell

I wake up one morning and to my shocking surprise

There wasn't a single cloud up in the lonely sky

The birds weren't chirping, the leaves all stood still

And to make matters worse, I received all my bills

My heart was telling me something, what I did not know

As a pain rush through my body, from my head clear down to my toes

My eyes started watering, the reasons I know not why

But deep within my soul, a big part of me has died

I called my fiancée, the operator answered the phone

She said the number may be right, but no one lives at that home

I drove over in a hurry, and yes I was amazed

To see the place so empty, it echoed like a cave

I woke up one morning and to my shocking surprise

There wasn't a single cloud up in the lonely sky

And when I gathered all my feelings up, I knew then

the reason why

My fiancée had left, without a single good-bye

My Mistake

How do I love thee… Off with your head

I saw you with another man, sitting on your bed

I thought we were inseparable, I thought our love was true

But in your eyes I can see, that I was the stupid fool

So please don't put me through heartache and pain

Just give me five minutes to explain

See, if I was to lose you now, I would lose my mind

Cause of all the ladies on earth, you are one of a kind

Now we both know it doesn't need to be this way

If this is called punishment, well you're really making me pay

Because without a doubt you're special to me girl

And you're the last thing I need to lose in this cruel world

So I will leave you two alone, to be with each other

What?...Huh?...Oh, why didn't you tell me he was your brother

Two-Face

They say you are a gentleman, and that you are a sweetheart

They mean you are a pest, and a waste of human art

They say your always there for them, and you lend a shoulder if they need one to

They mean they see you more than enough, and can't stand to be around you

You try your best to be outgoing, and to try and make new friends

And although they seem to be on your side, they'll stab you in the back in the end

The magicians use this term often, and so does the F.B.I

And stores use this to stop shoplifters, and to catch employees going awry

These people are called "Two-Faced", and they are as cold as Alaskan snow

And no matter how many times they smile at you, they hate your guts if the truth be told

There is no solution to this matter, you must come to work as told

The best thing to do is keep to yourself, and make no friends until your old

That way if they hate, dislike, or talk about you, you can turn your hearing aid down real low

Cause nothing hurt worse than to have a friend, and to find out they are really a foe

With friends like that who needs enemies, especially friends that treat you like dirt

So just stay to yourself, don't even speak to them, that way you will never be hurt

Still Choosing Life

Ladies and Gentleman, lend me your ears

For this important message that I want you to hear

A lot of people have told me; I need to show I care

About the situations that women go through, and the problems that they may bare

Maybe you were a victim of rap

And became pregnant by this crime

Or living in a s shelter, or on the streets, and can't afford a child at this time

Then turn your hearts to saving a life

Not destroying one out of fear

For there are couples unable to have kids of their own

And would welcome yours with happy tears

I know this child has not been born yet, so you must be its voice

Just remember you're here today because someone cared, so please choose to make the right choice

Thank God For Small Treasures

God has blessed me with many things, for which I am grateful for

He gave me life to start with, and a lovely wife for me to adore

A roof over my head to call my own, and a car for me to drive

A mom that I could never replace, and a father that I'm glad is still alive

The ability to finish high school and to stay in the medical career

But he could not bless me any better than with the child, my wife will soon bring here

A bundle of joy, a gift of love, to cherish and to hold

To teach and to raise into a healthy person, before we grow to old

To stroll down the street as a proud parent, or go to the park, or zoo

To buy stuff animals, and new clothes, to match the brand new shoes

Although it may not be easy I am sure we'll be just fine

With a little luck and patience, and a lot of love and time

Yes, God has blessed me with many things, for which I'm proud to say

That it is because of him that my heart soars, each and every day

And even though he did not bless me with power, fortune, or fame

I thank him for the little ones, to carry on the flame.

Your Man

As long as birds fly high in the sky, and tree leaves blow in the wind
And Grandmother's grab their grandchildren cheek just to see them grin
And bodies of water flow to shore, and meet to touch the sand
Rest well knowing that is how long you'll have me as your man

You see, my love is real and it is here to stay
And no one else can take that away
For as long as you'll have me, you will have my love to
And as the role of your man, my goal is to succeed in opening my love to you
Therefore, as long as there are stars in the sky, that looks down upon this land
Always remember until your dying days, you'll have me as your man

Leave It To Fate

If you go through life with that special someone, remember to treat them well

Because if you don't you just might lose them, and your life would be an empty shell

In a relationship you may quarrel and argue, those things do happen sometimes

And yes even with the best of couples, things may get out of line

It never was written in the book of love, that happiness is an easy task

There's not a doctor that can give you a potion, nor is there a person you can ask

My guess is the only way to make it work, is to communicate with your mate

And if it was meant to be it will happen, just leave it up to fate

K.T.F For Life

T.C.B was Elvis Presley's motto and there are quite a few who knows what it means

"Taking Care of Business" is what is stands for and he did just that so it seems

I to have a motto that I use in life, Which I share with the woman I love

It's K.T.F, and for me and my lady, it is perfect for the two of us

Even though right now we're miles apart,

I keep her close within My heart

And I know without doubt she's doing the same

Cause K.T.F is the link, in our unbreakable chain

You may ask what is K.T.F, does it come from a play or song

It's meaning shall remain a secret to my love and I, to keep our faith going strong

So until the day we are re-united, and I can make her my wife

It will be K.T.F forever, K.T.F for life

So when you read this, my dolphin girl, have no worries or strife

Dolphin's Casanova is here to stay, it's K.T.F for life

<u>If I'd Told Her No</u>

Staring into each other's eyes, with nothing but lust in mind

Knowing that we had all night, we decided to take our time

That early morning in the hotel room, we kissed and said our good-byes

As we headed off in different directions, to our husbands and to our wives

If only I had told her no, and turned and walked away

I would not be here now on bended knees, begging you to stay

You said the family that we built up, I had destroyed

in just one day

If I'd told her no then, I wouldn't be here now, begging you to stay

When I pulled into the drive-way, she was sitting on the front porch step

And she had taken out that old blue suitcase, from the closet, where it was kept

She stood-up with her luggage in one swift move, and with speed I've never seen

She slapped me with the back of her hand, and flung at me her wedding ring

If only I had told her no, and turned and walked away

I would not be here now on bended knees, begging you to stay

You said our love would have lasted a lifetime, if I had not gone astray

If I'd told her no then I wouldn't be here now, begging you to stay

No, I wouldn't be here now, watching you walk away

This World Would Be

This world would be a better place, if people had more love in their hearts

Instead of trying to hurt their peers, and rip their dreams apart

A better place this world would be

If friends could live in harmony

Where homelessness can never be thought of again

And drugs could be used for good causes, not sin

To go out in the world with a handicap or flaw

And not being laughed at by your peers at all

To have racism be a thing of the past

And unity was here to stay and last

Yes, this world could be better tis true

If it had more people in it like you

___Mountain…Get Out Of My Way___

Millions of people who gave it a try

Did not finish walking away without pride

Until one man came to try out his luck

At the task that was useless, that people gave up

He looked at the object and smiled in his own way

Yelling as he climbed "Mountain…Get out of my way!"

"He'll never make it" one man replied "It's far too hard to do it"

However, before they could blink, or wink an eye, what they couldn't do… he done it

People may say it can't be done, that it's as hopeless as a bottomless well

People may tell you that it is useless, and in the end you will fail

But just look at the object that you want to conquer, and set your mind to do it

And remember the saying "Mountain…Get out of my way"

And before you know it, you have done it.

Can You Feel The Love?

I can't help but feel this way

Whenever I think of you

My temperature rises, my body gets hot

And yet I'm shaky too

The palms of my hands become sweaty

My knees become real weak

Just the mere mention of your name

Makes it hard to speak

With plenty of air around me

Still can't breathe enough

Tell me do you feel it to

Can you feel the love?

Focused on whatever's at hand

Distracted at the same time

You make me sad, you make me happy

This feeling is blowing my mind

I go to restaurants starving

But can't seem to eat a bite

You're on my mind all through the day
And even more when I sleep at night
I know my feet are firmly on the ground
Still, feels like I'm soaring in the skies above
Am I the only one who feel this way
Tell me, can you feel the love?

Do Not Weep For Me

Do not weep for me
For I am not gone
Although my body may lay to rest
My spirit still lives on
When you feel a breeze upon your face
On a clear and windless day
Or see a flower blooming in the mist of weeds, in the month of may
When a shooting star lights up the sky, and the other stars seem to hide
Just know I'm there to share your experience, right there by your side
You see, just because you may not see me
Doesn't mean I'm not there
To comfort you when you need me most, with lots of love and care

Do not weep for me
For I am not gone
Although my body may lay to rest

My spirit still lives on
So whenever you start to miss me
Or start to shed a tear
Do not weep for me, my dear
I am still with you here

Tougher Than Nails

In this world we live in your bound to run across, a bully who wants a fight with you

They'll call you names and maybe shove you around, just to see what you will do

But before you swing that fist at them, before your anger brew

Remember another tough guy and ask yourself, what would Jesus do

They beat him, whipped him, and pulled out his hair, and not once did he raise his hand

But do not think even for one minute, he was any less of a man

Cause he showed them all that he was the toughest there was, when they nailed him to a cross to die

Then three days later he walked down the street, smiling with his head held high

Now don't you take my word on this, the bible told me this was true

Read it for yourself form people who knew him, like Matthew, Mark, or Luke to name a few

So when the moment comes and you feel you must fight, to protect your name on the street

Remember Jesus Christ, humble yourself, and turn the other cheek.

The Dilemma

When she walks into the room, your heart skips a beat

You can barely catch your breath, and mumble words are all you speak

You have brought her flowers and cards, and given her candy too

And the most you gotten are great big hugs, and a few polite thank you's

In your heart you believe you have a chance, but against you the cards are stacked

Cause it is hard to truly love someone, who does not love you back

She considers you the nicest friend, anyone could ever meet

And you'r the first person she would call, if lost down a dark alley or street

And even though she is quite single, deeper feelings for you she lack

It is hard to truly love someone, that does not love you back

Face with a dilemma, not knowing what to do

Rather to move on and find another, or keep trying like a fool

So you tell yourself she is bound to notice, sooner or later she will crack

And continue to show her your undying love, in hopes one day she'll love you back

Don't Say Good-Bye

She was five years old when dad and her, pulled up to her new school

And even though she'd said that she'll be fine, she couldn't keep her cool

Her eyes started to water, as she turned to look at dad

He couldn't help but smile, as he took her hand and said

You don't have to say the words, I can see them in your eyes

You don't want to leave this car, but this is not good-bye

I'll be right here, when school lets out, so sweetheart don't you cry

You don't have to say the words, I can see them in your eyes

Twenty years later, from a little girl to a bride, on this summer day

People are gathered in a park, as he gives his daughter away

The ceremony ended, and with tears in her eyes

She gave her dad a great big hug, and this was his reply

You don't have to say the words, I can see them in your eyes

And although your leaving to start your own life, this is not good-bye

You may be a wife to your new husband, but you're still my joy and pride

you don't have to say the words, I can see them in your eyes

Several years later, in a hospital room, there's a Dr. by the bed

He can see his daughter's lovely face, and the top of his grandkid's heads

Tears start to fill his eyes, cause he's too weak to speak

She can't help but smile at him, as she gently kisses his cheek and say....

You don't have to say the words, I can see them in your eyes

I know how much you'll miss us all, but this is not good-bye

We'll be together again in our other house, high up in the sky

You don't have to say the words, I can see them in your eyes

Just A Thought Away

Late one Friday night, while sitting on the hood of my car

I heard a familiar song on the radio, called "Keeper of the Stars"

I couldn't help but think of us, holding each other close

Telling one another in between kisses, "No, I love you the most

Or how you always wore that gorgeous outfit, when we were out on a date

And how your dad would wait by the door, if we were two minutes late

I remember our initials we carved on a tree, and put inside a heart

It is these things that keep me going, while we are apart

So when you're feeling down or even blue, because I'm not at your side

Turn on your radio when you're sitting at home, or even out for a ride

And if you hear that song by Tracy Byrd, that I used to sing to you

Just remember the good times me and you have shared, and it

will bring me one step closer to you

A Dream Come True

In 1968 a young black man, by the named Martin Luther King

Stood up in front of thousands, and said "I have a dream..."

He wished that every person, of every color, that lives under the sun

Would rise above prejudice, and come together as one

That hatred for the color of skin, would be a thing of the past

And unity for all races, would be in our nation to last

Mr. King lost his life, before he got the chance to see

The cause that he was fighting for, take a huge jump to reality

When one black senator from Illinois, decided that he would be

The one man to bring us together, for the sake of the economy

He became the 44th President of the United States, and it was Americans who made this so

As they came together as one voice, to help their country grow

And even though it took us 40 years, for this history to be made or seen

I'm sure Mr. King is smiling from heaven, as he finally gets to witness his dream

The Grey Soldiers

Like weeds around the house, you cannot just pull one

Cause once it is removed, others will surely come

They attack you without you even knowing, with perfect strategy

Two from behind, a couple behind the ears, and one in front for everyone to see.

Some may pop up and tickle your nose, and get to your cheeks and chin

Oh sure you can try to cover them up, but trust me they still win

Some may call it a sign of wisdom, coming in proud and bold

Others will tell you you're in denial, to face the facts you're getting old

Eventually they will take over your body and you will see them everywhere

Those navy-seal like attacking strands, better known as aging grey hairs

Home For Christmas

Mistletoes, and candy canes, and lots of presents galore

Santa and Frosty sits in the yard, and a wreath hangs above a door

There is ham and turkey in the oven, along with stuffing too

Everything one could want for Christmas, but what I want is you

I can do without the caroling, if your voice I could just hear

And to see you smile just for a few minutes, would bring me yule tide cheer

We may be miles from each other, but to my heart you hold the key

So please come home for Christmas my love, or at least by new year's eve

Flaws And All

In the years that we have been together, I've made my share of mistakes

Some have made you smile and laugh, and some has caused heartaches

Like never asking for directions, or leaving my clothes all over the floor

But you accept me flaws and all, and that's why I love you more

When others had given up on me, you extended a caring hand

And showed me that with self-confidence, I could be a better man

you know that I'm not perfect, by any means at all

And still you love me, unconditionally, in spite my flaws and all

So let people say I'm too clumsy, or too fat, or even a bit too tall

You love me because of who I am, unique, with flaws and all

In The Hood

Two young boys growing up in the hood, in the meanest parts of the streets

One hung out with gangs and thug, the other one class room's seats

One made his money illegally, by taking whatever he could find

The other made very little on his steady job, because he chose to further educate his mind

One guy is in a club, a fight breaks out, and gun shots started to fly

He shoots back effortlessly, but is still wounded by a stray to the chest's left side

His life is saved and he wants to thank the Dr., for patching him up so good

But is shock to see the man who saved his life, is the same guy from his hood

The morale of the story is simple, you have a choice you see

Just because you grew up in hell, doesn't mean your life will be

The hood doesn't make the person, you choose your own fate

What will yours be when you meet God, at the steps of the pearly gates

The True O.G

A guy runs around

With his pants hanging down

Throwing up signs with his hands

Fighting at the bars, and

Breaking into cars

Stealing whatever he can

He says "I'm a true O.G

As hard as I want to be

On my mama that ain't no lie

Don't get in my way, cause

With your life you might pay

That's just how we O.G's survive"

One day a stray bullet went by

And took the man's life

He stood in front of the man above

He said "I haven't been that bad

With the life I once had

So show this O.G. some love"

The man in white

Spoke very polite

As he shook his head instead of a nod

"You've been far too bad you see

And there is only one O.G.

*It is I, The **O**mnipotent **G**od"*

The Seduction

Into the candle lit room, I slowly creep

Where she motions me to sit and not to speak

I do as she ask and sit on the bed

As she stands in front of me, in heels and a dress of red

Down comes the dress, and as it hits the floor

Lower comes my bottom jaw, at the sight I've come to adore

She slips out of her heels, and the stockings come off

As I gaze at her lovely legs and skin, so smooth and soft

With a flick of her finger, to the bra's front clasp

From behind the lacy garment, the breasts are free at last

shaped to perfection, and silicon-free

With nipples lightly colored, for the eyes to see

The silk panties slide down, and a strip of hair is exposed

I cross my legs to cover, that which has arose

As my hands caresses her body above, and the heat inside down there

She lets out a moan, licks her lips, and give an erotic stare

I sit back to admire her, and to the angels above I must tell

If God had made anything more beautiful, he would have kept it for himself.

Another Try

I know the reason we're not together
Has a lot to do with me
Not being true and faithful to you
Chasing every skirt, I would see
But I'm getting older, and a little bit wiser
And more mature as the years go by
And I'd like to thank I'd be a better husband
When love decides to give me another try

I know it will not be easy
Nothing worth fighting for ever is
Money may stir up a few arguments
Now that I have more kids
But I'm not against working more than one job
And I've proven that in the years, that has gone by
So I think we'll be fine, if fate ever gave our love
Another try

On May 4th I said "I do" to you

You also told me the same

By the end of the day, when the guest went away

You were carrying my last name

Over a decade later you still have it

My guess is god knows the reason why

We are two people who are meant for each other

So let's give our love another try

What Goes Around

To dead beat parents around the world
Listen to what I say
Make time to be with your little ones
And show them you care each day
The adolescent years of a child's life
Are important in how they grow
Without and adult to show them wrong from right
How they'll end up only God knows
Selling drugs, in jail, or even dead on the streets
This and more is your reward, for being a parent who is dead beat
So when you decide to abandon your kids remember this fact or two
One day you'll be old and will need someone's help
And who do you think will take care of you

They Grow Fast

It was about ten o'clock, when I finally got to sleep

When I heard my newborn crying again, in a crib across from me

He tossed and turned and I could tell, it would be a very long night

My wife gave me a kiss and said, "It will be alright"

They don't stay little long, oh they grow so fast

Right now you're buying diapers, in large bulk and mass

But hang in there and trust me hun, even this too shall pass

They don't stay little long, they grow-up oh so fast

About thirteen months later, with a pair of brand new shoes

As he takes his very first steps, to Grandma and Grandpa too

He starts to wobble and bumps a counter, a glass breaks on the floor

I told dad I'm sorry about the cup he broke, he said "Don't worry

Cause I have more"

They don't stay little long, oh they grow so fast
Pretty soon the least of your worries with him, will be that
broken glass
He's barely walking, but give him time, this phase too shall pass
They don't stay little long, they grow-up oh so fast

Years later in the drive-way
His destination is the high-way
He kisses mom and dad and say good-bye
And when his car had finally disappeared
my wife can't help but shed a tear
and I look back on how, the time flew by

they don't stay little long, oh they grow so fast
a young man is driving off to college, in a Camaro full of gas
I remember holding him with just one hand, don't
Seem like that long has past

They don't stay little long, they grow-up oh so fast

Make time to be with your children, make memories that will last

Cause they don't stay little very long, they grow-up oh so fast

Forever And A Day

That special day in 2006, on the 6th, as I remember

You were brought into this world, in the summer of September

And every day my heart aches with pain, knowing I

Wasn't there

But it doesn't mean, not for one minute, that I do not

Care

You're my heart and soul, my joy and pride, the apple of my eye

And I love and miss you even more, on the days that

End in "y"

It warms the depth of my heart, when I call the house and hear

How excited you are to hear my voice, and "Da! Da!" in my ear

My time in prison is almost over, and I'll be home

soon to stay

So until then Hunter know that daddy loves you,

forever and a day

Remember The Time

Do you remember when five young brothers, dance and sung their way to fame?

And millions of people all over the world, knew their faces and names

Do you remember when the youngest one, did a movie with Diana Ross?

And started singing on his own, to become his own number one boss

Do you remember that shiny glove, he wore on his right hand?

And his infamous moonwalk he did on stage, that made everyone take a stand

From Beat It, to Thriller, to Rock With You, and to Billie Jean

He was a legend to millions in the faces that he came across and seen

So to hear the news on June 25th, that the King of Pop had died

Put the world in a state of shock, as they came together and cried

So to the family I give my condolences, because he was a beacon of light that shined

We will not forget Michael Jackson, we will forever remember the time

On My Mama

A young boy, still in my teens
Carried a gun, hard-core and mean
Representing the hood, I did my best
Walking with pride, demanding respect
    On my mama, it was no lie
    On my mama, I was the guy
Our rival gang, came to our town
And our posse formed, ready to throw down
Gunshots fired, from both sides
No cars on the streets, no place to hide
    On my mama, my aim was good
    On my mama, its one for the hood
Out of nowhere, a shot in the leg
One in the chest, and on the side of my head
I crawled to my house, mom came to the door
Just in time to see me, fall to the floor
Devon was my name, representing was the game
If only I had listen to mom, I'd probably would have had more fame

On my mama, is where I laid

On my mama, I died that day

Second To None

You are second to none
If I'd only seen that before
I wouldn't have turned to other women
I would have been at your front door
Instead lust got the best of me
And in weakness I did succumbed
I should have listened to my heart
You are second to none

You are second to none
No matter who stands in line
I may not always show it
But I've known it all the time
From the moment that I met you
I knew you were the one
No one else can come close
You are second to none

In a race to win my heart

Sweetheart, you wouldn't have to run
You could even crawl to the finish line
And still be second to none

Tribute To Mom

When I fell down or had a cut
You'd mend my wounds and pick me up
Gave me shelter and food to eat
Clothes to wear and a bed to sleep
Taught to respect my elders, and to be no fool
To study hard and to stay in school
When I was sick you took care of me, no matter how tired you got
It was you who took me to the hospital, when I had to get flu shots
Punished when I was bad, but praised when I did good
You're everything a child could want, and even more than he ever should
I can't say enough what you mean to me, but I hope this poem is a start
Of all the people I'll meet in this life, it is you who is dearest to my heart
I may not always show it, but I appreciate all you have done

I thank God for you every single day, I love you Mom...signed,

Your son

www.ingramcontent.com/pod-product-compliance
Lightning Source LLC
Chambersburg PA
CBHW071316110426
2743CB00042B/2648